COME OUT OF HIDING

DEDICATION

To my beloved parents,
Bishop Sean & Lady Julie Samuel:

You have been my first teachers, mentors, friends, and leaders. I am deeply honoured and humbled to call you Dad and Mum. Reflecting on the various phases and stages of my life, your unwavering love and belief in me have been a constant source of strength. Your pride in me has comforted my soul, and your words of encouragement have been a beacon of hope in times of despair. Your willingness to listen without judgment, even when my words were jumbled and my thoughts bewildered, has been a true blessing. The validation you've given me on countless occasions has empowered me to embrace my true self. If I can embody even a fraction of the love, wisdom, and grace that you both possess, I am confident that it will bring joy to God's heart.

With all my love and gratitude,

Naomi

FOREWORD

In almost four decades of leading, mentoring and developing people, it never ceases to amaze me how and who God chooses and use to fulfil his plan and to establish his purpose in the earth. Truly God is no respecter of person regardless of age, stage, ethnicity, class or gender. I have come to accept that God is too wise to be mistaken and too just to be partial in his dealing with us. Without exception, every new creation believer has been graced with a God given purpose with matching gifts and anointing. The scriptures bear this out, *"Now there are varieties of gifts, but the same Spirit; and there are varieties of service, but the same Lord; and there are varieties of activities, but it is the same God who empowers them all in everyone.* **1 Corinthians 12:4–6 (NKJV)** In a chance meeting with community champion and author Naomi Williams in the Spring of 2023, I commented (perhaps presumptuously) on what I perceived was her meek and unassuming demeanor. This sparked a conversation which at the time I had no idea how impactful and prophetic it wouldbecome. Our brief exchange about an obscure Old Testament prophet found resonance with Naomi and gave her a new perspective and insight into the purpose and gifts that God had given to her.

A year later under the inspiration of the Holy Spirit, what I thought was a passing remark in the corridor of the New Generation Church Community Hub in Nottingham, has materialised in a book. It gives me great delight to write the foreword to Come out of hiding, a book that is birthed out of a place of prayer and intimacy with God and written from the author's own journey from obscurity to an ambassador of healing, hope and transformation in God's Kingdom. *Come out of hiding* is a great resource for leaders and mentors with the responsibility of developing emerging leaders. It challenges deeply ingrained patterns and perceptions of people and their potential that we sometimes bring to our mentorship. It provides fresh lens to help us discern God's calling and timing for ourselves and for those who God has placed into our charge. An accompanying Purpose Journal is designed as an application tool to help the reader process the key concepts in each chapter.

In a generation where so many are hungry for acceptance, the dominance of social media with its power and persuasion is luring even the most reticent among us into the limelight. From the privacy of our bedroom we can now become an IG, Tik-Tok or YouTube influencer overnight.

Sadly, this is often at the expense of ignoring God's timing and season for our life and ministry. The truth be told, God is not interested in overnight sensation, wanna-be church celebrities or one hit wonders. I have seen first-hand where the premature exposure of gifted and anointment individuals has led to the miscarriage of their calling and the aborting of their purpose. The Psalmist caution us, *"It is God alone who judges; he decides who will rise and who will fall"* **Psalm 75:7(NLT)**

The lived experience of the author mirrors that of many biblical characters, women and men who were hidden between the pages of the sacred text, unnoticed by people but not hidden from God. I would even go as far as to posit that they were hidden by God in preparation for a set time and purpose. They were very much behind the scenes serving God faithfully and getting on with life. They were not necessarily looking for fame or notoriety and were sometimes even reluctantly brought into the spotlight. Check out Moses in wilderness, David tending sheep on the backside of the desert and Huldah the Prophetess hidden in the cloisters among the sons of the Prophets. One could say that they were hidden by God.

Come out of hiding is an invitation to men and women who are serving in obscurity, "hidden" and going unnoticed. Those who are secretly locked away from the glare of social media platforms and the attention of people who are oblivious to the gift and anointing that you are carrying. Get ready! God is about to bring you out of hiding for such a time as this. I declare that in this season, kings, priests and scribes will seek you out, not for your fame but ultimately for his glory.

Bishop Delroy Powell
New Testament Assembly –England
10-02-2024

INTRODUCTION
A NEW BEGINNING

In the naked scale of the tree, pain's sharpness dwells,
But does it soften when seasons change, as time swells?
Rain falls today, autumn's breeze stealing my cloak, Yet
I'll sway with the wind, winter's rhythm bespoke.

I cling to the promise of spring, the creator's grace,
Dancing amidst the whispers of this moment's embrace.
Each tear shed in loneliness, each leaf I've let fall, Adds
depth to my journey, standing tall through it all.

In the chill of winter's night, in the barren cold, I find
solace in knowing, spring's story yet untold. So as I
ponder on autumn and winter's embrace, I welcome the
promise of spring, a new life to chase.

*'For we are God's masterpiece. He has created us anew
in Christ Jesus, so we can do the good things he planned
for us long ago.'* **Ephesians 2:10**

For me to truly appreciate the space that I occupy, I must explore where I am coming from. I must know where I have been to, and I must know where I am going. However, digging into areas that have been laid to rest in not so much peace but just been laid, literally. It takes some uncovering, the uncomfortable exposure that leads to vulnerability in ways that are far from fun. You see, there is a reason I built a wall, although I may not have always known the value that Thee Creator had hidden in my very being, I did know how painful being misused felt. Note to self *it is important to be used for the purpose that I was created for otherwise I am allowing myself and others to abuse me.* Now, before we discuss me, I will set the scene. Let's explore the medieval landscape together, and I promise you the history lesson will be a useful one. All castles had surrounding defence walls. The Romans knew that every hideaway, above, around and within the defensive wall, would beinvaluable should their castle be attacked. I wonder what they believed was so valuable behind those castle walls that they were willing to give their last breath, which sadly most did leaving loved ones behind. I am not referring to a dignified and peaceful death either. The death in battle was instead that of a bloody and gruesome one, where the very air would carry the rhythm of grown men wailing and crying out in agony of the pain and suffering that befell them.

Soldiers screams would create an explosive melody carried by the wind to nearby people, helplessly waiting to discover whose victory had been claimed. Would they be closing their eyes tonight, to the same fate that lay upon their fathers, brothers and husbands. Or would they be closing their eyes a prisoner of war of a free *man*. Behind those castle walls. What was so valuable? Was it worth protecting? Why fight for it? The defensive walls, if constructed correctly, would provide safety from enemy fire and would allow nations to withstand attack. Some techniques adopted to build defensive walls were to make the base thicker to prevent the walls from being undermined and to allow for minimal damage from high impact. Not only did the defensive wall provide a sense of safety and security, but it also gave defenders the capacity to move around the city quickly and hidden areas to fire arrows. Usually, the opposition were unaware of their enemies, who had little, if any, chance of fleeing before being struck.

Exploring the defence system of medieval times shed light on the time and effort I had put into creating such a wall around myself. My fortress kept me hidden from the painful messages of enemies and allowed me a sense of safety and security behind the gates locked across my heart. The reality of being hidden was something I resented.

I had created this tomb as a safe space not realising that taking root in the thicker baseline of my defensive walls was discouragement, self-doubt and unbelief. It is incomprehensible that I genuinely thought I was driving in the direction my life was headed, by responding in ways that had become my default settings. Someone had cut an essential wire, and I was no longer connected to the source. So, I would take out my bow and arrow, put on my helmet and get ready to defend my territory. I would vow, never again, it could never, I would never, they can never. Not realising while I was busy creating a false sense of security, God was putting a hedge of safety around me. At times, I'd find the hedge like a glass ceiling that only I could not seem to progress past. It is rough seeing everyone around you excel as a Christian and then to feel unseen to such an extent that you would outlive your sins only to be still paying compensation for each one long after 'time served' was up. 'Tis a shame. If only I had known that being hidden in nature was God's way of wrapping me up to allow me time to work on myself from the inside out. To reveal to me the value of each gift and how to truly implement purpose as it was intended. However, much like a child thinking they can see the complete picture, I was reacting off one part of my reality, not understanding anything about the other ninety-nine per cent and wailing like those Romans in agony from a bloody, gruesome and slow death of my soul.

BROKEN CRAYONS STILL COLOUR

When I was a child, I loved to be creative. I would watch a wellknown children's programme called *Art Attack*, where the artist used recycled materials to create the most amazing pieces of art on a massive scale in a football field, for example. Saturday mornings would be cereal, art attack and melting custard creams in front of the gas fire. While contemplating replicating the artist's masterpieces in my parent's kitchen. I would pull together cardboard, Sellotape and crayons that would see me through some of the day's events. You see, as young as I was, probably no older than six or seven, I knew my sibling's rubbish was my treasure. I could make something out of nothing that would keep me occupied in my imagination, falling over into Sunday. I found my joy and creativity dampened as time went on, and the expectations on me eroded the walls that I had built, and the pressure caused them to crumble. I felt vulnerable and angry, I am unsure when anger took root where innocence and optimism had once resided, but it would later blossom into a poplar of resentment that would take at least six truckloads to remove. Fast forward to 2022, when I was colouring with my three-year-old son. He said, *"We can't use those crayons, Mummy"*, I asked him *"Why"*. He responded, *"Because they're broken, they need to go in the bin now"*. I swiftly replied *"No, Kai look"*, as I rushed to save every snapped and dishevelled crayon as if giving them another chance somehow helped me feel better as it was a similar turn of events that I had once longed for, *"Broken Crayons Still Colour"*. *"Okay mummy,"* and just like that he accepted it, I was able to exhale. I could not help but think I wonder if even at three this lesson will become one that he grows up believing in. One I had wished that I'd believed just enough to know that in my brokenness I was still valuable instead of believing the lie that I had been forgotten and discarded.

There have always been two narratives at play in my life. I can look back and see moments of clarity and encouragement as I pursued victory in Christ Jesus, as well as the sting of the harsh reality that plagued my life where I just was not good enough, holy enough, submissive enough, meek enough, but rather too loud, too honest, too sensitive and just too much.

I would hear through the grapevine that people would pass remarks such as *You know what Naomi is like.* When unbeknown to those very people, I was trying to figure out what I was *like*, so I am not sure how they knew. All of that said, God is indeed the Chief, and He orchestrated my life in harmony, the quirks that knit together my character make it so beautiful that I now believe in imperfect perfection.

OVER TO YOU.

Embark on a journey of self-discovery, where the echoes of rejection fade into the background, and the melody of acceptance begins to play. Picture a tapestry of emotions, woven intricately with threads of revelation and courage, unfurling before your eyes like a canvas waiting to be painted. In the depths of your being, confront the shadows of the past with a courage born of discomfort, knowing that each step forward brings you closer to the truth of who you are. Peel back the layers of doubt and despair, revealing the strength and resilience that lie beneath. Imagine yourself surrounded by walls, not as barriers to keep you confined, but as fortresses of protection and strength. Behind these walls, discover a sanctuary where you are free to explore the depths of your soul without fear or hesitation. As you navigate the labyrinth of your past, let each moment of vulnerability become a stepping stone towards healing and growth. Embrace the discomfort of uncovering old wounds, knowing that in facing your demons, you pave the way for a brighter tomorrow. Reflect on the innocence of childhood, where broken crayons are not discarded but cherished for their beauty and resilience. Find solace in the simplicity of self-expression, knowing that even in your brokenness, you possess the power to create something beautiful.

Look back on your journey with a sense of clarity and encouragement, knowing that every trial and tribulation has led you to this moment of triumph. Embrace your uniqueness, knowing that you are fearfully and wonderfully made by a Creator who orchestrates every detail of your life in perfect harmony.

CHAPTER ONE
HIDDEN IN PLAIN SIGHT

'Now more than ever I believe that the work started when your eyes were first uncovered to the truth that you have a saviour, that you need a saviour and that you love the saviour, must be swiftly completed in you'. The Bible notes a telling message from the book of Hebrews 10:25 (NLT). *'And let us not neglect our meeting together, as some people do, but encourage one another, especially now that the day of his return is drawing near'.*

The day of the Saviour Jesus Christ of Nazareth continues to come closer and you have work to do. It is personal, this is something your inner being has been screaming out for long enough.

It is difficult because where do you start when there are years **IT IS PERSONAL** of pain, decades of suffering and time has become the opposite of the healing ointment that it was promised to be?

So I ask you as I once asked myself, have you ever felt like you do not know what to do? Have you ever felt like you have not got this? or like you could not see how it would all work out? Maybe you have felt like there was no seat at the table. Or this path you are treading you have never seen it being done before? Maybe, you have cried through most of it and lost the words once uttered in prayer. You are still finding your way, and trying to hold on? Has there been times when your sick and tired are sick and tired? You always need reassurance? Have you not been able to trust God beyond knowing, can you see where you found yourself putting up barriers to protect yourself? If any or several or all of those experiences resonate with you then this is the book for you! Roll up your sleeves because you have got work to do. To be hidden in plain sight is to be unnoticeable, by staying visible in a setting that masks presence. Roll back the film that plays in your mind, to those uncomfortable memories where you have truly felt unnoticed. Where were you? What was happening around you at the time? Why were you not able to be seen? I wrote a poem once when I too felt completely unnoticed it is printed in my book *Shattered* entitled *Now do you see me*. The words of a young women who was yearning to be seen, stung by her reality that no one really knew the turmoil within her even existed. As she would have a front row seat to so many other's stories not really ever being revealed as the starring role in her own story. A story that seemed insignificant and hidden. It is strange when you know you are there but you are not really there. Everyone knows you but they do not take the time to really read the words of your heart and explore the whirlwind which is your mind.

If you have ever been in a room full of people and not had a defined presence or purpose you have probably felt extremely uncomfortable and disconnected. Usually, invitations to places and spaces that amplify the very fact that you are unimportant become easy to say no to or not even to bother sending an R.S.V.P. at all. Maybe the invitation was a matter of politics and not really about having you there in the first place. Rejection is a cruel pill to swallow because it can make you truly believe that absolutely no one cares about you and then it will find ways to prove this theory time and time again until that is the only narrative nursing your wounds. On the outside, you see, nothing has changed, you either show up and play the part- dancing to the rhythm of the room, or you make an excuse and rid yourself of having to play the merry-go-round of small talk and fake smiles altogether. Because who would really want to spend the entire time looking at the clock and the exit as if it were a game show and you needed to make it through that rectangular shaped hole across the room, to complete the round and win the prize of misery and loneliness once again, but hey it could be worse you could actually enjoy the interactions, maybe even find a sense of self and begin to swim in a place that has been a swamp of dirty laundry usually you sinking in your dirty laundry laid bare for everyone to see. So they can say they saw you there, therefore you were there right? But did you participate?

Were you a part of? Was there a real sense of belonging? It is easy to show up, to look the part and be seen without really ever being noticed. Is that the game plan show up and look the part? When my son was three years old he would always ask me to play hide and seek, he loved this game *"Mommy I will hide and you find me"*, although he had not quite grasped what the word hidden really meant. He would hide, usually somewhere that was easy to find him and always in the same spot (under his quilt cover) and then he would giggle and wriggle around the bed while I walked around his bedroom after a lengthy and animated count down. Shouting "Now where is he", rummaging through the draws and other furniture around the room. Eventually I would get to the bed, pretending that I hadn't heard him giggling and telling me he was over there. To his delight and amusement, I would play the role and be so shocked that I had tried to sit on the bed for a rest and realised that it was too bumpy only to find him hysterical with laughter that I had sat on him "by accident" now at aged four he has mastered the art of hide and seek and can often go unnoticed while peering through the flap of the clothing rails in the shopping centre, this time not to my amusement. I wonder which you are. Are you likened to a child who is frantically trying to remain hidden not wanting the pressures of being seen or are you truly hidden peering out beyond the darkness and isolation, in such a public place that it is shocking that you have never been noticed. If you are either or none of the aforementioned, take note that God knows exactly where you are. With God, you are in plain sight, like Adam and Eve in the garden, even when trying to hide, even when God asked them where they were, He knew, and He made a point of asking to demonstrate that they had made every effort to hide parts of themselves from their creator. Adam and Eve, the first humans in the Bible, lived in the tranquil Garden of Eden. Adam, created from dust, and Eve, from Adam's rib, enjoyed a harmonious life, tending to the garden and communing with God. However, tempted by a serpent, they ate from the forbidden Tree of Knowledge. This act of disobedience opened their eyes to good and evil, leading to their expulsion from Eden and beginning humanity's journey of struggle and redemption. I wonder how it felt to be so proud of something that you created and wanted to showcase it to the world only for it to decide to hide parts of itself. What are you hiding and where are you hiding it?

I wonder if the issue lay deeper than that if you are someone who has somehow lost their way in the chaos of life. When I was a child, I used to go to my grandma's house and meet up with all of my cousins, the adults were piled into the living room and the kitchen was out of bounds to children, so we often found ourselves playing on the stairs.

There would be up to eleven or twelve of us at times decorating the stairs with our socks, snacks and juice boxes fun times! I remember vividly a game we used to play called Chinese whispers, no idea where the name came from and as an adult, it doesn't quite make sense. The rules of the game were that one person would whisper in the following person's ear and so on, and the last person would say what they thought they heard out loud and usually this was not the version that was initially whispered leaving us all in fits of laughter as we rolled around the stairs, with tears dancing down our face. I pose the question who has got your ear? This can often be the one who is telling the narrative that keeps you hidden in plain sight. Maybe distorting your story and perception of what God has placed within you. Speaking poison which is killing your dreams and destroying your hope. Who has got your ear? Are they suffocating you from the inside out? leaving nothing left to be rescued following the battle with one's self. I wonder who truly has your ear and are they re-traumatising you maybe replaying those memories that hand you another brick as you build that wall of protection around you? You see trauma is real, but trauma is also subjective, subject to the individual because one person can experience the event and skip away without a second thought, whereas another person could be stuck in the same event long after the experience and be completely broken by the trauma itself. Your experiences, your genetic make-up, your personality, your morals, your beliefs and your perspective on your experience play a role in how traumatic it can be.

Can you get so distracted by what is around you that you lose sight of why you began? Of course. It happens all the time, Bishop Sean Samuel once preached a word *it's only a shadow*, it is something I remind myself of now whenever I notice distractions looming. They are not real, just shadows, they appear larger than they are, more powerful than they are and are there as a figure of darkness distracting me from why I started. Bishop Sean Samuel, the elected Bishop to the New Testament Assembly (NTA), is a gifted preacher an expert in biblical exposition, an evangelist, a church developer, and a prayer intercessor. He is a loving husband and father and a kind- hearted person with a keen interest in serving humanity. He co-founded the New Testament Assembly New Generation Church (NTA NGC) Nottingham in 2006 and was appointed as its Senior Pastor by the late Bishop David Greaves in 2009.

Through NTA NGC, he has successfully guided and empowered numerous young people from diverse socio-economic and cultural backgrounds, enabling them to discover their potential and contribute positively to society. He is a passionate and skilled preacher with a strong focus on teaching and deliverance. He is deeply committed to serving the Christian community with humility and integrity. Over the years, he has had the opportunity to spread the gospel of Jesus Christ in several countries, including Ghana, India, Antigua, Jamaica, and the United States of America.

There is an old story told about two arrows, one arrow causes the initial pain but the lasting pain is the second arrow. The second arrow is often the rumination, the over-thinking, the cascade of catastrophic thoughts following the event that causes the most pain and trauma. You have a choice, to be hit by life just like the first arrow, this is something out of your control after all life comes hard and fast and usually blindsides you. Or to feel the lasting pain etched in you until it becomes a part of your very make-up by standing, waiting and expecting the second arrow to completely unveil yourself leaving yourself laid bare, with no protection as the second arrow pierces your hope and your dreams. Typically, when deciding especially one that is long term such as the decision Lot made in the Bible can have consequences of its own. Do you know what the decisions that you make today? Such as where you decide to put down roots, can impact your culture, your family and the whole generation that comes after you. Some things in life can look so pleasurable and pleasing to the eye but when they get into you, things can quickly turn ugly and start to erode at the inside cavity walls of your heart and mind, this is when it can be difficult to get rid of them. It is always worth sticking with individuals that can teach you something or share nuggets of wisdom with you. This can be the difference between pain and suffering rather than excelling. Proverbs 13:20 *'Whoever walks with the wise becomes wise, but the companion of fools will suffer harm'.* When Lot was given the option to choose a place for him and his family to live, he did not pray about it and he did not ask those that were wise around him. Instead, he chose what looked good, what was pleasing to his eyes and tickled his desires. The place that he chose was not hidden, I can imagine it drew a lot of attention, a lot of revenue and a lot of travellers looking to do things to fulfil human desires, lusts, and most definitely exploits that they would not be caught doing in their home, their life and especially not their day job. Hidden in plain sight!

I wonder what you have chosen, look back over the choices that you have made. Do they bring you or others pleasure? If you had a chance to lay them bare in front of you, could you easily find confidence that they were decisions based on and for the will of God?

IT IS TIME TO UNVEIL THE WORK WITHIN.

Amid life's chaos, where pain has been a constant companion and time seems to mock your healing process, the journey ahead can appear daunting. Yet, amidst the uncertainty, there is a stirring within, a call to action that resonates with the depths of your being. Perhaps you have felt invisible, longing to be seen and understood in a world that often overlooks the depth of your existence. If any of these experiences resonate with you, know that you are not alone. This journey of self-discovery and healing is a personal one, but it is one you are called to embark upon with courage and determination.

To be hidden in plain sight is to exist without truly being seen, to wear a facade that masks your inner turmoil. Yet, beneath the surface lies a yearning to be acknowledged, to be embraced for who you truly are. As you peel back the layers of your past, confronting the moments of pain and rejection, you may uncover wounds that have long been buried. But it is in facing these truths that you find the strength to heal and grow. Like a child playing hide and seek, you may find yourself frantically hiding from the world, afraid to confront your vulnerabilities. Yet, in God's eyes, you are never truly hidden. He sees you, He knows you, and He calls you to step out from the shadows and into the light of His love.

Trauma may leave scars that run deep, shaping your perceptions and influencing your choices. Yet, in acknowledging your pain, you take the first step towards healing. For it is in your brokenness that you find the strength to rebuild, reclaim your narrative, and embrace the fullness of who you are meant to be. In the midst of life's distractions and temptations, you are reminded to stay true to your purpose, to stand firm in your convictions, and to walk alongside the wise. For the decisions you make today have the power to shape not only your own lives but the lives of generations to come. So, as you reflect on the choices that lie before you, may you find the courage to follow the path that leads to life and wholeness. And may you discover, in the midst of it all, that you are never alone, for God is with you every step of the way.

CHAPTER TWO
TRAPPED BY YOUR OWN HIDING PLACE

To be hidden is to be kept out of sight and concealed. I wonder why you have been kept out of sight, I wonder if there was a purpose in the concealment of your very existence and I propose a thought stream that I hope to put forward but we will come back to that shortly.

Now that you have recognised the possibility that you may have been hidden in plain sight. I wonder if you can reconcile with the notion that maybe just possibly you are trapped. By walls meant to keep you safe, bars that stop others from coming in have ultimately restricted free movement and growth. The type of growth that you thirst for, that seems intangible because of the memory of a sharpness that continues to prick the very core of hope that you cling onto.

Life can often throw you some of the worst curveballs that you were never going to be able to catch. Even with the best intentions it was just never going to be straightforward. In the Bible John 16:33 refers to suffering in this life. I guess the one thing you are promised with your first breath is suffering. Right?

I know, I know it is very depressing and I have not even gotten to the best bit! Because in 1 Peter 5:8 you are warned that your enemy, the devil, is constantly prowling like a roaring lion, literally looking for who he can devour. So although you can feel blindsided and like the troubles of life just come out of nowhere, I can see in the scripture that God pretty much prepares you for the pain and suffering to come.

What do you do when it all gets overwhelming? I can feel you as I write these words, as ink is penned to paper. I feel you flicking through the window of memory. Remembering what overwhelms your heart and what brings your soul pain. I feel the lump in your throat and your eyes welling up, as you make the split-second decision on whether to keep reading or not. I encourage you that to be able to, maybe just this time, try something different and see what happens. You see, to others it seems that you are a swan gracefully moving on the water. The sun cascaded across the tapestry of the silk, white masterpiece. As the water ripples while you glide through with sheer grace. Hmmm or so it seems to others. When in reality even a swan has to put in a tremendous amount of effort to stay afloat. To not sink beneath the terrain of the waters. What one does not see is the flapping beneath the water as the swan desperately swims. What is keeping you flapping earnestly beneath the surface?

Feeling overwhelmed is joined heirs with hopelessness that have the right to depression. You do not need a doctor to tell you that you are depressed. You have stopped taking part in daily life that once gave you purpose. You not be motivated for social pursuits that you used to enjoy. You take longer to respond to others not for lack of time but for diminished connection. You feel sad all of the time and you cannot seem to shake it long enough to feel the familiarity of happiness. You may even be venturing on a trodden path that you thought no longer existed or if it did you had put up many of warning signs and barricades to ensure that you never ever walk the path of 'suicidality' again. However, it is back again, the uninvited guest at your dinner table. The heavyweight and the dark cloud that seems to rain only over your head and your life. Where is that sunshine that you were promised? The freedom to live a life in abundance and favour. You know, all of that good stuff about Christianity that is belted from the pulpit time and time again. Human psychology lends itself to explaining what happens to your brain when you have met with what feels like a dangerous scenario and you need to protect and preserve yourself. This is known as fight, flight or freeze. Fight mode is straight defensive, you kick off and do as the word means you fight and you fight with everything that you have got. Flight mode is saving yourself from even facing that giant and running away as fast as you can and without a second thought. Freeze mode is the in-between it is like not knowing what to do and become so overwhelmed by fear that you are paralysed and cannot respond. There are physiological responses that let you know that you have switched into default mode. These responses included sweating, a fast heartbeat, crying, wetting yourself, not being able to talk, panic attacks or shortness of breath and an impending sense of doom. Do you know what your default setting is and has it been freeing or limiting?

It is easy to mask this feeling of being trapped. On the outside you can look very happy, maybe I could even go as far as to say that you appear content. You demonstrate a calm demeanour that fools even you for a moment. Masking is tough because it takes more energy to pretend and to keep up the pretence, especially when it feels like the walls are caving in and you are struggling to find your way out of a very bad situation.

Usually, depression is associated with sadness, lethargy, and despair for example, it could be someone who cannot make it out of bed. Though someone experiencing depression can undoubtedly feel these things, how depression presents itself can vary from person to person. I cast my memory back to the early days of practising as a social worker, I worked with a family, and on the outside, the whole family appeared very well put together, happy and *'normal'.* However, once the review was away and I was just conversing with the parent, I asked a question, 'What is a typical day in the life of...' and with that, the walls meant to keep out professionals like me came crashing down. She was in tears, sobbing uncontrollably; she shared how she has clinical depression, is in bed all day has agoraphobia, and has not left the house in 6 years. She has tried to keep this from her youngest daughter and so will put clothes on just before her daughter comes home from school and pretend, she has run errands all day. However, her eldest daughter would have done all the tasks needed to keep this façade going. I used graded exposure and set realistic targets, first, she was able to have a wash and stay downstairs for a few hours after her daughter went to school, then say goodbye to her daughter at the front door, then the garden gate and eventually walk with her to the end of the road. She commented on feeling like she was suffocating for so long and this change had help her feel like she could breathe again and get the help that she needed for her mental health and her family, she had truly taken off the mask.

I came across an interesting theory that I would like to share with you. *'Smiling depression'* is a term for someone living with depression on the inside while appearing perfectly happy or content on the outside.

Their public life is usually one that is well put together, maybe even what some would call a normal or perfect life. Smiling depression is not recognised

SMILING DEPRESSION IS SOMEONE LIVING WITH DEPRESSION ON THE INSIDE WHILE APPEARING PERFECTLY HAPPY ON THE OUTSIDE

as a condition in the Diagnostic and Statistical Manual of Mental Disorders (DSM-5) but would likely be diagnosed as major depressive disorder with atypical features. Does any of this ring true? Internally there are changes in appetite, weight, and sleeping, fatigue or lethargy, feelings of hopelessness, lack of self-esteem, and low self-worth, loss of interest or pleasure in doing things that were once enjoyed. Outwardly you may be an active, high-functioning individual. Someone holding down a steady job, with a healthy family and social life. You could be a person who appears to be cheerful, optimistic, and generally happy.

Have you ever felt ashamed of something that you have done or been a part of? Feeling ashamed is momentary, whereas, carrying the burden of shame is debilitating and can lead to unforgiveness of self. This, in itself, is a prison that not even a heavyweight in the kingdom of God can get through. Not your pastor, reverend, priest, bishop or church sister or brother. The work to release yourself from unforgiveness of self is only something that you can do.

It takes a special type of repentance, deliverance, surrender and restoration and only when you have done all this with the Holy Spirit will you truly be free from the trappings that once held you bound. The Bible notes very clearly in Zachariah 4:6-9 that no amount of willing, wanting, nor power can do it. I challenge you to try a different way instead of trying to force the pretence of freedom. Try it for real let go of shame and go along the undignified journey of forgiving yourself. Of course, you first need to be honest with where you are at currently and where you have been. There was a time in my life when I felt so stuck in a hiding place that I had once made my entire existence. But suddenly as the days progressed the hiding place felt as though it was becoming smaller and smaller. I remember why I had banished myself to the deepest darkest valleys and although everyone else had appeared to move on I just couldn't quite shake the external condemnation and the internal shame of feeling that I had missed the mark several times over. So, it was easy to hide until it was not. As life went on, I could feel the tug of God to go deeper, I knew what my purpose was and every so often I would dip my toe in it but not enough to be totally committed. Just enough that I was still connected, in a fashion, but could pull out easily if necessary. Just before being completely overcome by the pain of rejection. It never really worked as you may have figured out by now.

If an arrow is coming for you it somehow becomes magical and develops superpowers in turning corners, going through walls, and piercing you anyway. Well, this is what I had found and because I had shut everyone and everything out I was left to do a botched job in nursing my own wounds.

Fast forward to a time when I discovered that the people in your circle can be very useful and often crucial to how you face a battle and the outcome. A few years ago, I experienced something that will be etched in my memory forever, but that is a story for another day and a different book! What I want to share with you is how it literally knocked the breath out of me. I physically could not grasp air, reality and life. Everything felt distant suddenly and everyone was intangible. The people around me became my saving grace as in times before. For prayer, for those messy tears and for comfort. The Bible refers to the blessing of wise advice and being able to seek out wisdom from the right people in Proverbs 11:14. Thank God for people who look beyond the mask of perfection and see the fragile human and the broken heart. **So back to you**, your priorities must align with where you believe you are heading. Having misplaced priorities is like the old saying *"Do as I say not as I do"* it gets you nowhere.

There is a place in God where you can learn to silence the internal noise.

The chatter that keeps you up at night. The grumbles that stop you from ever really laying your head to rest in the first place. But remember to really do this you need to be wise about where you choose to set down those roots, wise not only for yourself but for your family as well.

The decisions that you make today will ultimately be the life or death of your legacy. There are principalities and rulers of darkness attached to places and spaces and you need to be aware of spiritual fortitude when scoping the landscape for a relationship, a career, a ministry, a home and financially just like the example of Lot in the Bible, who chose to reside in a place that was pleasing to the eyes only to later regret the impact that had on his wife and daughters. When meditating on the life of Lot and the decisions that he had made, a term gripped my very being *'Excellent Grace'*. Living in excellence is a pursuit that requires relentless determination. Grace is given by God through His son Jesus Christ of Nazareth. Therefore, it was pertinent that at this point in the book you are reminded of an excellent grace gifted by your Heavenly Father. So, what happens when the place you once felt kept you safe, the perfect shelter from the storms of life? A space just big enough for you, within the walls that you put up, what happens when they start to become suffocating and instead of keeping you safe, they start to become a hindrance in moving forward like an enemy of progress! Imagine being trapped by your own hiding place. Thank God for Jesus because a little further along in John 16:33 Jesus encourages you to be strong in heart because he has overcome the world. So, I wonder and I hope that you will catch this train of thought with me. Do you really need to remain trapped behind the prison walls that you put there? I think they have served their purpose, don't you? Is it not time to step out of survival mode and see what you can do when you are not wound up to fight or run and hide? I wonder what peace looks like for you. I wonder what freedom looks like to you. I wonder what hope feels like for you. I wonder what salvation does for you.

CHAPTER THREE
HIDDEN IN PLAIN SIGHT

Imagine knowing that there is more to your current situation but not knowing how to live freely. Seeing others doing it and possibly having a sip of the same freedom when you delight in their company but not knowing how to make it stick. Freedom looks good on them; I wonder if it'll suit you too! It can get like that sometimes where you are so consumed by living a life chained by decisions, bound by actions that you do not see a way out. In a well-known UK newspaper, there was a headline 'Britain's hidden scandal the disabled people trapped in their own homes'. How does a place, particularly a space that is called a home, which is supposed to be a place of security and safety become a prison? Dare I mention the dreaded 'C' word! A couple of years after the newspaper article was published, the covid-19 pandemic swept the world and suddenly, every individual realised the stark reality of what it felt like to be housebound. For at least one year the nation was shut in and confined. Individuals were not free to move about in their daily lives as before. Policing every single movement a person made became the norm and fear across the country stifled every household. It was no surprise that the symptoms of the said virus seemingly attacked the lungs and airways.

Breathing became increasingly difficult for many and even those deemed healthy were suffering from the backlash of a new variant that spread rapidly across the globe. It was a silent killer, an unseen disease, something that became a phenomenon, leaving many in states of panic and pain. Alongside the impact on health and the economy, we witnessed the mind becoming traumatised, the children suffering from isolation and adults powerlessly experiencing relationship breakdown. Mental health and safeguarding referrals increased crippling an already full social care and healthcare service. The teams in place to support individuals were too busy trying to tend to their own lives, losses, and injuries. The world had moved into an international state of emergency, and no one knew the extent of the crisis nor when it would all end. The term 'a new normal' started to rapidly take shape, if the world should begin to understand that there was no going back but a change in how people would live. Many became content with the new normal and began to adjust. For some individuals that I worked with, nothing had changed because they were already in a state of being 'locked in'. Locked-in syndrome is a rare disorder of the nervous system. People with locked-in syndrome are: Paralysed except for the muscles that control eye movement. They are conscious and aware of their surroundings. They can think and reason but cannot move or speak; although they may be able to communicate by blinking and eye movements. Are you 'locked in'? Does it feel like you are trying to live in a new world that feels foreign to you? Have you ever watched a film where the person gets stuck in sinking sand? You usually find yourself holding your breath and gripping the arms of the couch, hoping that they'll survive. However, you see panic set in and as they move trying to free themselves, they seem to become even more stuck. Often the more you thrash around in a desperate attempt to escape from your own situation you can become stuck and continue to sink. I do believe that the decisions that you make today can and will impact a whole generation. You serve an all-seeing and all-knowing God but you chose, in one desperate attempt to save yourself or maybe to protect yourself, to hide away. I had planned a family day with my husband and children, we had two children at the time. Our eldest daughter had decided that she would be the DJ for the duration of the fifty-minute drive. At first, we did not mind but there was only so much rap and drill on repeat that one could take while responding to the toddler asking, *"Are we there yet?"* Every ten minutes. I said, *"Alright that's enough, I'm changing the song now"* and in response, my teenage daughter said, *"Mum you're an enemy of progress".* We all burst into a fit of laughter. It was such a teenage thing to say! But it made me think. Are you an enemy of your progress? What are you stopping yourself from doing?

How are you hindering yourself from growing?

ARE YOU AN ENEMY OF YOUR PROGRESS? Perspective is so important when making decisions about your future. If you have been through a difficult time and have not experienced healing, you can often live from a traumatised place. Trauma can change your outlook on the path you have taken and the way you see yourself and others. Imagine looking at yourself in a broken mirror, the image is distorted no matter how long you look or how hard you try to think it differently. Until the lens 'the mirror' is fixed the image will never change and you will not be able to see or accept the blessings and miracles of God in their purest form because you are looking through broken glass. It is crucial at a time like this in your life that you know how God sees you when you have felt invisible when you were rejected, when people underestimated your ability, and when you have been devalued or humiliated by those that you loved.

Conversely, there is another set of people feeling completely overwhelmed by the calling of God who are walking along a road that has never been walked before. You have never seen anyone in your family, or your community do what you believe that you have been called to do. You feel as though you are an imposter, and this is creating fear and doubt where faith and hope once resided.

It is as though you need to get your shovel out, roll up your sleeves, and start forging the way not only for yourself but for those who will also, one day find themselves in the position to move beyond the limits and boundaries that once held them captive. God could not find even ten righteous people to save in Sodom and Gomorrah, but Lot found favour in God. God sent angels to save Lot and his family before the city was destroyed. It is crucial to know what the appropriate response is at the opportune time; this can be a game changer for you and your family. Sometimes this requires following God without knowing where the path leads, where the resources are coming from, and where the help is. Maybe you are reading this, and you feel that you do not need convincing you have that sincere hunger for more but you are still 'housebound' and cannot seem to get unstuck long enough to remain free. What is your posture? Galatians 2:20 *'20 I have been crucified with Christ and I no longer live, but Christ lives in me.*

The life I now live in the body, I live by faith in the Son of God, who loved me and gave himself for me'. Living in total surrender is a daily choice, possibly a daily battle. I always think of it as it's Me vs. Me that is the real war. A total surrender to Christ Jesus helps keep me in a posture of peace and hope. It does not make it easy but there is no place I would rather be. It has been a war and a half!

But it is well and I know that if I have felt like this, I am pretty sure some of you may have too. I encourage you today to choose to live with an expectation. To give every burden and doubt over to God. To receive peace and hope or whatever it is that you need from God Himself. Picture yourself totally lifted to the heavens head up and arms wide open. It is amazing because it signifies not only surrender but also empty hands that have an openness to receive what God has. I wonder if the person reading this is crying, worshipping, sobbing or silent. I wonder what your posture will be before God today. Being able to go before God with prayer, praise and stillness is a powerful space to hold. Not every battle requires noise, even silence is powerful. You may be familiar with the song 'It is well' this hymn was written after traumatic events in Spafford's life. By 1870, Horatio Gates Spafford was a successful Chicago lawyer with every reason to be thankful and faithful to God. A supporter of preachers Dwight L. Moody and Ira Sankey, prominent Christian evangelists formed part his circle of friends. The first series of unfortunate events was the Great Chicago Fire of 1871, which ruined him financially (Spafford had been a successful lawyer and had invested significantly in property in the area of Chicago that was extensively damaged by the great fire). His business interests were further hit by the economic downturn of 1873, at which time he had planned to travel to England with his family on the *SS Ville du Havre*, to help with D. L. Moody's upcoming evangelistic campaigns. In a late change of plan, Spafford sent the family ahead while he was delayed on business concerning zoning problems following the Great Chicago Fire. While crossing the Atlantic Ocean, the ship sank rapidly after a collision with a sea vessel, the *Loch Earn*, and all four of Spafford's daughters died.

Spafford's wife, Anna, survived and sent him the now famous telegram, *"Saved alone ..."*. Shortly afterward, as Spafford travelled to meet his grieving wife, he was inspired to write these words as his ship passed near where his daughters had died. Bliss called his tune Ville du Havre, from the name of the stricken vessel (written by Lyn Williamson, 2024, on eden.co.uk). Can you in your current situation state that it is well, can you muster up the courage to mutter those words? Carrying the burden of mistakes is a heavy burden to bear. When you know of God, you know what your mistakes are, and you can often feel the shame of these shortcomings. Furthermore, what if you are carrying the burden of what someone else did to you, how you were ultimately rendered hopeless and now you crave to fill that void time and time again? Sometimes the very thought of doing something different can be debilitating remember how your mind responds to stress, fight – flight – and freeze. There is triggers inside of you to help you to survive but when survival mode keeps you stuck, you must step past that default setting. What about being stuck by the bars of your past by decisions? By the limits that others placed on you. Or knowing that things should be done differently but trying to convince others of this. Change is not going to plan. You do not look like what they expect the change to be. Maybe they do not want to hear it from you. I am often named as a disrupter in the workplace, disrupters are suspicious of the status quo and constantly seek ways to stay ahead of the game. They are intellectually curious and keen to understand changes in the external environment and in the minds of their consumers. Additionally, I am known in the church as a spearhead, to initiate, launch, prompt, and spur. Both descriptions of my character are one and the same, they speak to the passion and drive that I have for fairness, change, and justice. So, it was opportune when I was offered the chance to study at the doctoral level in a university leading change for mental health and neurodivergence. However, not everyone was supportive of this change. The head of the service had asked, why does someone like Naomi need a PhD? Although the words left a sting, I remembered a prophecy spoken over me in 2018 about my life and the impact I would have internationally. But as part of that impact, I would feel the hit of breaking down walls and barriers. I am now in year two of my doctoral studies in mental health & neuroscience, I have never seen it being done before.

I have no idea where it is all leading to, but I can honestly share that stepping out of my comfort zone feels good. I have excelled already, and I am ahead of where is expected, being given opportunities I could have only dreamed of and have in parallel to this journey been elected as Vice President for an international youth mental health organisation. God is truly faithful, and you may have read some of my previous books to know that I was hidden and that did not matter to God. You have the power to break free from any chains holding you back. Embrace change, step out of your comfort zone, and pursue your dreams with boldness. Believe in your potential and trust that God has a plan for your life. Your past does not define you; it is the courage to move forward that shapes your future. Be a disruptor, a spearhead of change, or connect yourself to one! Then watch as doors of opportunity swing wide open. You are capable, you are worthy, and you are destined for greatness.

CHAPTER FOUR
THE REVELATION

There is something about being up high that impacts on perspective. Suddenly, you can see more of the landscape and how it all beautifully intertwines. How the tapestry of the day cascades across your world and meets the same effect of the night. The was no mistake when the Bible referred to an eagle when demonstrating the magnitude of strength that we are gifted Isaiah 40:31 *'But those who hope in the LORD will renew their strength. They will soar on wings like eagles; they will run and not grow weary; they will walk and not be faint'*. Eagles have a powerful vision. Eagles are fearless. Eagles are tenacious. Eagles are high-flyers. Eagles nurture their young. Lot was regarded as a righteous man! (2 Peter 2:8) Lot did believe God and because of his faith, God did save him. He was not a perfect man or even close to it. His conduct was influenced by the people he lived with, but God saw fit to justify him. Now this does not sit well with me but is that not so like people? We pick and choose who gets God's forgiveness and grace. God is not like man in any way and I for one am so grateful for that.

Revelation can be defined as 'the divine or supernatural disclosure to humans of

THE DIVINE DISCLOSURE OF SOMETHING RELATING TO HUMAN EXISTENCE something relating to human existence'. I believe in God's divine intervention, and I know that for complete and lasting change God must intervene. Not many people will make it to the revelation of who God called them to be. Fewer will be able to live out this revelation with a mind made up, heart wide open, and a total surrender to the Creator. In Matthew 22:14 Jesus states that *'many are called but few are chosen'*. To be able to hear the call of Jesus Christ is to silence the noise around you. The chaos can often become so loud that you are unable to make space to truly listen to the voice of God. I wonder what God has been trying to say to you. I wonder how long God has been trying to get your attention. Is it possible that you have been so busy for busy's sake that you have missed the very essence and simplicity of solitude by laying completely at the feet of Jesus? In Luke 10:38-42 the Bible refers to Mary who laid at the feet of Jesus listening and soaking up the wisdom, knowledge, and anointing. It is important to note that as Mary lay there her sister Martha rushed around doing the day-to-day serving but with a begrudging heart.

She believed that Mary was somewhat lazy and not helping her with all that needed to be done. There is a time and a place for everything and a season to do and a season to be both seasons complement each other, and you must be aware of what season you are in.

In the doing season you *sow* into what you believe to be God's purpose for your life and the lives of others, and this is a valuable process as you will later reap what is *sown.* So be generous in *sowing* because this will one day mature just like premium bonds, shares or savings and become greater than the original seed. I love the scripture which refers to not resenting the day of small beginnings (Zachariah 4:10), it rings true! I encourage you to nurture your small seeds, water it and watch it grow. The process of learning to be, now, many do not get this invaluable lesson and it is in fact a process that must be learned. In a world where busy is the norm and a badge of honour. You can often feel guilty for simply resting, being still or allowing time for solitude. There is a whole movement now around self-care, ensuring that people give time and space to taking care of their physical and emotional well-being. The term self-care is just another notion for what the scripture refers to as resting in the bosom of Jesus Christ (John 13:23), to be in the position of rest just as a child does as they lay completely at peace in the arms of a parent is invaluable. To be chosen by God is another word for being elected, the elect of God is a powerful term.

When applying for the role of Vice President I had not imagined that I would be chosen by individuals of great intellectual and educational calibre. This gave me a feeling of being valuable although that feeling was temporary because humans cannot fill the space designed for how God sees me, but it is a glimpse into what it feels like to be chosen by God. Knowing how God sees you is what I call a game changer because suddenly you see yourself through the eyes of the one who created you. You can get a deeper understanding of the quirks and mechanisms of how you were meant to be in this world. That is truly special, furthermore in 1 Peter 2:9 the Bible notes *'But you are a chosen people, a royal priesthood, a holy nation, God's special possession, that you may declare the praises of him who called you out of darkness into his wonderful light'*. Imagine if you let this scripture truly soak into your very being, pierce past the hard shell of your heart until it penetrates all the lies, pain, anger, trauma, and hurt and the words soften you. I know it is scary to be vulnerable, I know they hurt you and I know you vowed never to feel the pain again. I challenge you to feel it, be triggered, and be vulnerable but do it in the safety of the shadow of the almighty God your Jehovah Shalom, in His bosom because in God there is a peace that will allow you to see the mess and not panic. You will be able to wear the scars and no longer feel the pain. This stage of the journey is a part of the healing process and allows you to become whole. This part cannot be skipped or rushed and is crucial for the place God has for you to occupy. A few years ago, I decided to take up running, this was something new because if you knew me before then you would know that this is the last thing I would decide to do in my spare time. I started with the couch to 5k and after nine weeks of dedication and discipline, I was able to run 5k in just over thirty minutes. I was so proud of myself and after joking with my brother-in-law found myself very quickly running my first 10k, which also happened to be on the first day it had snowed that year. It was freezing, it was icy but the feeling after achieving my first 10k in one hour and seven minutes was exhilarating. I was beaming, I had pushed past my comfort zone, I had ignored the doubt in my mind, and kept going. Putting one foot in front of the other, slow and steady, while remembering to inhale and exhale. I managed my body temperature throughout the run with gloves on and gloves off. It truly was an experience that I will never forget. I was able to encourage my brother-in-law to keep going and he was able to encourage me. The cars sped past us, cyclists rang their bells to alert us that they were heading our direction and people stared in disbelief that we had decided to run at minus temperatures when we could have been more comfortable by a warm fire with a hot mug of tea! Ecclesiastes 9:11 *'I have seen something else under the sun: The race is not to the swift or the battle to the strong, nor does food come to the wise or wealth to the brilliant or favour to the learned; but time and chance happen to them all'.* I share the details of this run to give you a tangible example of the journey that you are on.

To know the revelation is one thing but to step into that revelation and not look back, remember Lot! Well although God showed compassion on him and his family. Unfortunately, Lot's wife was tied to something in the city, something in her past and she could not get free from that hold. So much so that it caused her to look back when they were leaving, and she turned into a pillar of salt (Genesis 19:26). It is interesting that it was salt that Lot's wife turned into. Salt is something used to season food or enhance flavouring when cooking. The Bible refers to you as being the salt and light of the world (Matthew 5:13-16) to be encouraged to be all that you were created to be. There are so many reminders and encouragement within the word of God and even placed inside of you. I believe that as you have been reading the words of this book you have found that it is relatable and more so that it has started to fan the flame which once burned bright in your heart and life.

Of course, it can mean getting messy and offering undignified praise, worshipping before the feet of Jesus (2 Samuel 6:14-23), being that open, unashamed, testimony of the goodness and grace of God. Or maybe you will be the one wailing before the feet of your Lord and Saviour (Jeremiah 9:17) moving the heart of God on behalf of your salvation and the salvation of your family and community.

You might even find yourself laid out prostrate in total surrender (Genesis 24:52), bowing before God the maker of heaven and earth. However you meet the Creator is personal to you and God, I encourage you that as the day of Jesus' coming draws closer to find the revelation that God placed in you and live. Have you ever noticed that depending on your perspective on a task will usually depend on how you tackle it? If you believe the task is easy then you are more likely to go for it and give it your best shot. Whereas, if the task ahead seems difficult then you are likely to procrastinate, maybe say you will do it tomorrow or come back to it later. Typically tasks which are left for another time start to become a burden and seem like a far bigger task requiring more effort and energy than originally expected. I have a to-do list which typically has everything and anything that I need to do. Some things on this list take less than an hour, others will take a bit longer maybe a few hours. However, there are things on my list which are far bigger tasks and will take months. With the larger tasks in my to-do list, I have noticed that if I do not break them down into smaller chunks and make some form of daily, monthly or weekly target reminders to do a part of it, then they become too overwhelming, and it takes so much longer to complete. When I mentioned to someone that I was writing this book they asked me if it was a self-help book. I paused and thought about it. I do not think that this book is merely a self-help, *ten steps to a newer freer you* book, that will fill you with excitement and great ideas but not push you to make the changes needed. I believe that this book has started to unpick some things in your heart, mind and soul that you thought you had dealt with. Parts of your journey that you do not mention nor cast your mind to. Not because of any reason other than time has passed and you believe that you have moved on. You see, part of the revelation is allowing God to flick the lights on in those darker more ugly places and as God does *this* He will work on *that*. God will allow you to be whole even in the places that no longer exist in your present day, nor do you expect them to exist in your future. Because God is a God that is not limited by time He will go back and heal you in your past, right now, so that He can hold you in your present, as you step over the threshold into the newness of your revelation in Him. This new place has no room for residue that triggers you. It has no space for reminders of past traumas and torments of mistakes that bound you for so long. You have cried, you have had your sleepless nights, and you are ready for your new beginning (Isaiah 43:19). Your journey toward revelation and self-discovery is an extraordinary adventure, guided by divine intervention and the call of the Creator. Embrace the whispers of your soul, for within them lies the essence of who you are meant to be. As you navigate through life's ups and downs, remember that you are chosen, valued, and deeply loved by a God who sees your potential beyond measure. In the pursuit of your dreams and aspirations, do not let the noise of the world drown out the gentle voice of your calling. Take moments of solitude to listen, to reflect, and to align your heart with the purpose set before you. Like Mary at the feet of Jesus, allow yourself to be fully present, soaking up the wisdom and grace that surrounds you. Yes, there may be challenges along the way, moments where doubts creep in and fears threaten to hold you back. But remember, you are not alone. With every step you take, with every obstacle you overcome, you are being moulded into the person God created you to be. Trust in His plan, for it is a plan filled with hope, purpose, and endless possibilities. Therefore, embrace the journey, dear friend. Embrace the highs and the lows, the victories and the setbacks, knowing that each experience is shaping you into a stronger, more resilient soul. As you press forward, may you find courage in the knowledge that you are a chosen vessel, destined for greatness in the hands of a loving and faithful God.

CHAPTER FIVE
THE POWER TO CHANGE THE NARRATIVE

In Judges 6:12-16 you will find part of Gideon's story, a biblical hero, begins as a timid man hiding from the oppressive Midianites. After asking for signs to confirm God's divine call. Gideon's journey from doubt to faith showcases how God can use the most unlikely people to achieve great victories. He thought that he was a nobody. He stated to God that he was from the least essential tribe of Israel, the least important family, and the least important in his family. He was the least of the least of the least. One day, he was in the process of separating the wheat from the chaff in a winepress. This was unusual as a winepress was a deep hole in the ground that was lined with stones. Typically, it was used to juice grapes to make wine, not to thresh grain. Threshing removed the chaff and stalks from the grain, which was the only edible part, through the process of stomping on the wheat. This was always performed outside because the wind played an important role in blowing away the chaff. Usually, this was done in a field, but here was Gideon, hiding in a winepress. Why? It is questionable that he possibly did not want to be seen by the Midianites. He was scared and so found himself doing the unusual, making himself occupied with something that was not his role nor necessary instead of facing the fear that kept him hidden. I love though that God knows where you are even when you believe that you are hidden! While Gideon was busy hiding, an angel of the Lord appeared to him '12 *The angel of the Lord appeared to Gideon and said, "The Lord is with you, mighty warrior!" 13 Then Gideon said, "Sir, if the Lord is with us, why are we having so much trouble? Where are the miracles our ancestors told us he did when the Lord brought them out of Egypt? But now he has left us and has handed us over to the Midianites." 14 The Lord turned to Gideon and said, "Go in the strength you have and save Israel from the Midianites. I am the one who is sending you." 15 But Gideon answered, "Lord, how can I save Israel? My family group is the weakest in Manasseh, and I am the least important member of my family." 16 The Lord answered him, "I will be with you. It will seem as if the Midianites you are fighting are only one man."...'.* As the scripture continues, Gideon needed a lot of convincing that he was the person for the assignment and that God had not confused his capabilities for someone else. Eventually, he surrendered his thoughts of how he perceived himself enough to trust and obey God's request. Resulting in Gideon triumphantly leading the Israelites to defeat the Midianites. Erwin Raphael McManus is the lead pastor of Mosaic, a mega church based in Los Angeles. Erwin is a speaker on issues related to post-modernism and postmodern Christianity, and also writes and lectures on culture, identity, change, and other topics. He wrote about the importance of storytelling, *'The Christian faith grew through story, not text. Only later did the stories become Scripture. While the Scripture must be held in the highest regard, we must not neglect the power of story.'* The word narrative is often used by the media, politicians, and commercial enterprises. They understand the power of the narrative, which can be used to spread a message, cultivate emotional connections, and control a story in the cultural landscape, in fact, narratives shape culture. Stories have a profound effect on people, from a single individual to the widespread masses. Can you think of a good storyteller? When my husband tells a story he will focus on every detail of the narrative and make sure that it is accurate. If not, he will retell it until it is a true reflection of the event. I, on the other hand, will coast over important details, exaggerate, and make the story as animated as possible. We could both be recounting the same story, but you would never know it by the difference in our delivery. A good storyteller will have the balance between the key facts, draw on the imagination, and introduce humour, they will ensure that the story is emotive and captures your heart. The story would be theatrical and will leave you with a lesson that it teaches. For instance, can you remember a testimony that has always stuck with you or that changed your mind about a struggle, a situation or a perspective on something? Revelation 12:11 *'They triumphed over him by the blood of the Lamb and by the word of their testimony'*. A good testimony, story, or narrative has the power to change policies and processes. The Interesting Narrative of the Life of Olaudah Equiano, or, Gustavus Vassa, the African (1789). Equiano's autobiography was published to coincide with the May 1789 parliamentary debate on the slave trade, and clearly influenced politicians and the public. His book became the most popular and widely read. A story creates bonds with one another, it is how we relate to each other, and how we find connection with people. A story heals, sharing your story, acknowledging the journey, and releasing it from being this thing that causes you to stay tied up has the power to trigger the process of healing. By relinquishing shame and embracing God's grace. Think of some names or roles that you have been labelled, both the welcomed and the not. For example, wife, mother, daughter, friend, aunt, colleagues. *'Labelling theory refers to a theory of social behaviour which states that the behaviour of human beings influenced significantly by the way other members of society label them. It has been used to explain a variety of social behaviour among groups, including deviant criminal behaviour'* (Howard S. Becker, 1963). Think about a deeply horrible, painful thing that has been said to you or that you have heard.

A self-fulfilling prophecy is *'a false definition of the situation evoking a new behaviour which makes the originally false conception come true'* (Robert k. Merto, 1968). When our beliefs and expectations influence our behaviour at the subconscious level, we are enacting what is known as a self-fulfilling prophecy. It begs the question, what is your internal belief system? How does it feel when you believe the negative things that were said to you and they become your narrative? Do you know that beyond that narrative will be a divine narrative over your life gifted to you by God? What could God be saying to you? What could you not be hearing amidst all the noise and negativity that has spread like weeds in an unkempt garden? It's time to prune, to cut away and to clean up. Proverbs 18:21 suggests very plainly that *'death and life are in the power of the tongue'*. The story we tell others about ourselves often reinforces the negative narratives. Where does your story come from does it tell of the authentic you? Do you feel yourself sharing a narrative that even you do not like? In Proverbs 23:7 it is noted that *'as a man thinks, so he is!'* This is the story that you tell yourself. Usually, there is a huge contradiction between the story you share with others and the narrative that is going on in your head. Masking is a natural coping mechanism and survival trait from experiencing undue stress and pressure. Survival mode is typically rooted in fear. Read an excerpt from my book Shameless by Naomi

Williams *'I missed the mark 17 x 7 times, at least! and for that I hold myself to account, I've locked the door and thrown away the key. My mind replays every moment of what I have done, and my heart has become cold to the very hope that more can be fulfilled with this vessel. After all I am dirty, I am unclean, I am broken, and not enough heavenly glue could fix me. Guilt has me bound, the words above keep replaying in my mind, over and over again. I am not enough, I am worthless, I am just stupid...stupid...stupid. Why have I nternalised negativity, guilt has swept me off my feet and is carrying me along a current of destruction. Guilt is building walls that even my loudest praise cannot tear down. These solid, iron-clad walls lock me in and lock everyone else out. Maybe that is all I am good for, making mistakes, I haven't even got the strength to resist. So, I give into this thing that church people call lust, pride, control, and manipulation. I always think I've got it under control until it is too late. My head feels like it's going to explode, I cannot seem to get the bad deeds that I have hidden in secret to stop replaying in my mind. If I can see them then how do I pretend they are not there? How do I say to all these people God saves, he forgives, and I am made new? It does not even feel right, and I do not even believe it really, well if I did why would I keep doing the things that I do not want to do and not doing what I think is right, what I think is just and what I think is of God.*

I carry around masks and each mask is for an occasion.

My work mask shows the world of education that I am strong, I am independent and I am in charge. My church mask shows the world of Christianity that I am perfect, I am free and I am at peace. My family mask shows the world of close relations that I am happy, I am loving and I am super-mum.

But I am not any of these things really, not on the inside, I hate myself, I hate my life and I am so tired of holding it all together. I have been through so much and having to keep holding everything together is exhausting. Especially when there are a lot of people who are not fans of me already, they are constant reminders of my mistakes and they make it so very clear I am no more than that of my mistakes. I am no more than the process I went through to find who I am. This just stirs the pot even more, why do I have to be filled with guilt anyway, if I knew better, I promise I would have done better. The me I am now is not the me I was one hour ago; well I think not. It is so hard to promise to be better because it is easy to promise when I feel good but when I feel my back is against the wall, I slip and fall again. Straight into what put me in this mess in the first place. So, I have no idea what to do now, all I know is what I have done before and that is not working because I keep finding myself at the same destination and no further than when I started. Maybe I should just settle for what my life is, I think I have tried and I do not really believe I deserve any better anyway. It is strange though, because even though I have this overwhelming sense of guilt, I am still search-ing. There is a part of me which is not quenched and until I find what it is that can quench this thirst, I think I will continue to search. I do not really know what I am looking for, I know what I have been told, I know it is Jesus, but I do not know Jesus.....'

Your story is closely linked with your Identity. What would your first response be if some-one said, I would love for you to come and sing at our concert you have such an amazing voice. Or if they were to compliment you on how beautiful you are. Maybe share how much they learned from you and how brilliant you are at doing your work. Some of the narratives could read like this

IF THE WORDS THAT YOU THOUGHT ABOUT YOURSELF APPEARED ON YOUR SKIN, WOULD YOU STILL BE BEAUTIFUL?

Narrative = I am not good enough
e.g. I don't believe any good will come of it always goes bad in the end.

Narrative = Self-sabotage
e.g. you will get in there first to ruin it because even a good thing will go wrong in the end it always does.

Think about your narratives and what thought patterns they have stemmed from. So, you are ready to come out of hiding you are starting to emerge as we move through the text together. How do you go from labels that you are given your whole life resulting in narratives which are permanent fixtures in your mind? To this notion of living, moving, working, walking and speaking in a narrative that is all you have known your whole life. It is a process; in 2015 I went through a radical change in my life, I declared war on my thinking, speaking, behaviour and actions. I wanted my past to no longer influence my present or my future. You must try something different to get different results. I believed that my purpose, *'although others could not see it, and why would they I had made a bit of a mess, so if track records were anything to go by my predictions for the success of any form were low'*...however, I believed that I had a purpose if only I could get God to use me. It meant becoming extremely vulnerable and open to change. Picture this, your life as you know it, getting completely turned upside down until everything was shaken out and then being placed the right way up again. I was totally empty and ready to be filled by God, a process is a series of actions or steps taken in order to achieve a particular end. Now go back to that list of narratives that you have in your mind and think about your purpose, your goals and your aims in life. How could you get there?

What one small action can you take to change the outcome? For example, one goal I had was to have healthy relationships, the process to reaching this goal was that I read every book on relationships and learned what God said about them. The outcome was a rejection of the narrative that I was not enough and an embrace of the narrative that I had a lot of love to give and deserved love too. Leading to God's purposed narrative of healing in past and current relationships and a healthy marriage. You have the power to change the narrative in your life. I was speaking to a young person and they said *"I just deeped it and I look at what some people in my family have turned out like and I am not here for it, that just can't be me"* at that point I smiled, I said you can choose your narrative and the conversation continued. There was something profound about that conversation, for that teenage girl. She had looked around her and decided that she was destined for greater, purposed for more, and that she would not settle for less than what she believed was for her. Dr Grace Lordan wrote in her book Think Big (2023) *'The power of our own narratives to shape both our actions and inactions is tremendous'.*

Therefore, I want to shed some light on the forgotten hope that once rang loudly in the streets of your heart and mind. Where there is what once was but now only a shadow of happiness. It takes just one! One moment in the presence of God, one reflection on what could be different next time, one conversation where you soak up genuine narratives. One decision to believe the truth in your story and one action that effects permanent change. In Philippians 4:8 the scripture encourages us *'Finally, brothers, whatever is true, whatever is honourable, whatever is just, whatever is pure, whatever is lovely, whatever is commendable, if there is any excellence, if there is anything worthy of praise, think about these things'*. Your journey towards self-discovery and transformation is an extraordinary adventure, guided by divine intervention and the call of your Creator. As you navigate life's challenges, remember that you are chosen, valued, and deeply loved by a God who sees your potential beyond measure. Yes, there may be doubts and fears along the way, but you are not alone. Embrace the highs and the lows, the victories and the setbacks, knowing that each experience is shaping you into a stronger, more resilient person. So, embrace the truth, embrace the hope, and embrace the journey towards a

CHAPTER SIX
THE UNVEILING OF SELF

newer, freer you.

I did not know that I was me! Sound familiar? The Bible talks about rejecting thoughts that you have about yourselves. It is questionable if there is an understanding of who you are before you go through the process of unveiling in front of others. The unveiling of self is like watching a cocoon slowly crack open, revealing the vibrant butterfly within. It's a mesmerising dance of transformation, where layers of doubt and fear peel away like autumn leaves, unveiling the true colours and intricate patterns of one's essence. Each moment becomes a brush stroke on the canvas of existence, painting a portrait of authenticity and self-discovery. As the veil lifts, the soul emerges, fluttering with newfound freedom and radiance, ready to soar into the boundless sky of possibility. I recently attended the *'Northen Ballet Romeo and Juliet'*. There is an excitement of being a part of the richness and creativity within the walls of the theatre, coupled with a sense of nervousness of the unexpected. It was all new, I had thought about what to wear for the last couple of weeks. We needed to try it was not the typical joggers and t-shirt occasion. I spoke to those that I was attending with only to conclude that this was not our average affair we needed to dress as though we belonged there.

Acknowledgement is like stepping into a grand theatre before a captivating performance begins. As you take your seat, you glance around, taking in the ornate décor, the hushed murmurs of anticipation, and the velvet curtain veiling the stage. Each element whispers a story of what is to come, inviting you to acknowledge the rich tapestry of experiences waiting to unfold.

Just as the spotlight illuminates the stage, acknowledgement shines a light on the intricacies of your inner world, inviting you to embrace the journey of self-discovery with curiosity and openness. Picture yourself standing in a vast library filled with books representing the layers of your identity. As you explore the shelves, each book whispers secrets about who you are. You pick one up, feeling its weight and texture, acknowledging its significance in the story of your life. Sitting in this depth of acknowledgement while meditating on the word of God and the gentle whispers of the Holy Spirit declaring every good and perfect thing that God created you to be. This becomes the fuel needed to burn the flame of your soul brighter than one can imagine. When I was a child, I used to love being outdoors. I would chase chickens, and dig up worms, I spent hours just enjoying the fresh air and freedom from boundaries, away from the typical mundane and routine behind the walls of a home.

Discovering the terrain of the landscape and soaking in the crispness of nature was life to my core. I vividly remember catching butterflies with my father, and admiring them in a jar before releasing them and setting them free. I could do this for hours! The beauty, and fragility of the wings always intrigued me. The butterfly, a delicate masterpiece of nature's design, dances gracefully on fragile wings, each delicate stroke a testament to its ethereal beauty. Its wings, like stained glass windows, gleam in the sunlight, adorned with hues of sapphire, emerald, and amethyst. As it flutters among the blossoms, it becomes a living poem, weaving through the tapestry of a garden in full bloom. Yet, beneath its fragile exterior lies a quiet strength that belies its dainty appearance. With determination and resilience, the butterfly emerges from the confines of its cocoon, breaking free from the bonds of its past to embrace the boundless sky.

YET, BENEATH ITS FRAGILE EXTERIOR LIES A QUIET STRENGTH THAT BELIES ITS DAINTY APPEARANCE Each beat of its wings carries the weight of transformation, a reminder that even the most fragile creatures possess the power to defy gravity and soar to new heights. In its fleeting beauty and ephemeral presence, the butterfly embodies the essence of life itself, fragile yet resilient, fleeting yet eternal. It whispers secrets of metamorphosis and renewal, reminding us to embrace change and celebrate the journey of transformation, for in the delicate wings of a butterfly, we find the strength to embrace our own evolution. I used to thirst for stillness, a quietness in my soul that moved me from a low, destructive and downcast place. I would find myself stealing those moments and making every effort to hold onto them for as long as time would allow. Allowing myself to get caught up in the dance of thoughts that would decorate my mind when noticing a rainbow. Remembering what it represents, as my body filled with a gush of hope. The flooding of memories that transported me to that very moment of where I had come from. Words would fail me but a smile and kiss to the heavens would be the least of my demonstration of gratitude. Reflection is akin to standing on the shore of a tranquil lake at dusk, watching as the setting sun paints the sky in a symphony of colours. As you gaze upon the mirrored surface, you see not just your own image, but the echoes of your thoughts, feelings, and memories rippling across the water's expanse. Each ripple reveals a fragment of your inner world, reflecting the depths of your soul in shimmering hues of gold and indigo. In this moment of quiet contemplation, you become both observer and participant in the dance of your own reflection, allowing the gentle waves to reveal the hidden treasures within. Imagine sitting by a tranquil pond, watching as ripples form and distort your reflection.

As the water becomes still, see your reflection becoming clearer, revealing hidden depths and nuances. Dive beneath the surface, exploring the underwater world of your subconscious mind. I wrote a poem entitled *'Waiting to Exhale'*, as pain can often cause you to hold your breath. It is time to breathe, let go of the inward breath and release all of the doubts, the fear and the anxieties. Breathe in an outward breath and allow the Holy Spirit to flow through every facet and chamber of your life. Acceptance is like the soft glow of dawn, gently illuminating the horizon with hues of warmth and promise. It is the silent surrender to the ebb and flow of life's currents, where each wave carries whispers of peace and understanding. Like a river carving its path through the landscape, acceptance carves a channel through the heart, allowing emotions to flow freely without resistance or judgment. It is the tender embrace of a loved one, wrapping you in a blanket of unconditional love and support, or inviting you to rest in the sanctuary of your own truth. Visualise yourself in a serene garden, surrounded by a variety of flowers in bloom. Each flower represents a different aspect of yourself, from the brightest blooms to the thorniest vines. Embrace them all with open arms, recognising their beauty and value in shaping who you are. I remember making a defining decision in my life and at that moment it did not feel very relevant to a different way of life. I felt the opposite and instead was very deflated and was filled with a deep sense of sadness. I was grieving for what I thought I wanted and what I had lost. The next morning was a Sunday and come hell or high water on Sundays I would go to church. So that morning was no exception, however I did not attend skipping and dancing. Rather I swallowed the lump in my throat and made the paces forward that led me to the doors of the building. When entering each step started to feel heavier than the last and I was quickly regretting my decision, the one it took years to have the courage to make. The one that would change normality as I knew it. Suddenly the singers raised a song to the rooftop of that building that silenced my doubts and lightened my steps *'my soul says yes Lord yes to your will and to your way my soul says yes Lord yes, I will trust you and obey when your spirit speaks to me with my whole heart I'll agree, and my answer will be yes Lord yes'*. They sang it at the top of their voices with conviction, it felt like a declaration as the drums beat and the congregation clapped. It was then that I knew the divinity of the moment that I had stepped into. The release is like a solitary leaf detaching from the embrace of a sturdy branch, drifting gently on the autumn breeze. It is the exhale of a weary traveller, letting go of heavy burdens that no longer serve a purpose, feeling the weight lift with each breath. Like a bird taking flight from its nest, release is the liberation from self-imposed cages, spreading wings wide to explore the boundless expanse of possibility. It is the whispered mantra of surrender, echoing through the corridors of the mind, inviting freedom to flow in like a river carving through stone.

Create a sacred space in your mind, envisioning it as a cluttered attic filled with boxes of old beliefs and expectations. With each box you open in prayer, feel the weight of past conditioning lifting off your shoulders. Throw open the windows of your soul in total surrender, allowing the freshness of the Holy Spirit and the light of Jesus Christ to flood in, clearing away the cobwebs of doubt and insecurity. Integration similar to a symphony of diverse instruments coming together in perfect harmony, each note blending seamlessly to create a masterpiece of sound. It is the art of weaving threads of experience, wisdom, and emotion into a rich tapestry of understanding and wholeness. Like a puzzle coming together piece by piece, integration is the process of aligning disparate elements of self into a cohesive and unified whole. It is the dance of joy and sadness, love and loss, as they intertwine and complement each other in a delicate balance of existence. I had been so isolated and set apart from this life, my community, and the world for almost sixteen years, that it was well over a decade that I had lost myself in the shadows of lies about who I was. Picture yourself with the Master weaver, sitting at a loom with threads of every colour imaginable.

With skilful hands, weave together the threads of your experiences, passions, and dreams, creating a tapestry that reflects the complexity and beauty of your true self. Allow God to mould you into the vessel of honour that you were created to be.

Integration can create a symphony of diverse instruments coming together in perfect harmony, each note blending seamlessly to create a masterpiece of sound. It is the art of weaving threads of experience, wisdom, and emotion into a rich tapestry of understanding and wholeness. Like a puzzle coming together piece by piece. I once made a decision that was believed at the time to be extremely risky. I left my full-time, flexible, secure, minimal-stress job to set up an organisation in the community. To make ends meet financially I would do agency and consultation work which gave me the flexibility to be available for the demands of building a business. I prayed and declared to God while driving home one afternoon, *"I believe God that this is your will, and you will pull me back to catapult me forward"*. I felt the fear, I heard the advice that maybe I should keep my job and juggle until it was stable. I ignored it all and did it anyway! I am pleased to say that eleven years later the company is sustainable and still running. There have been difficult days, months and years but when I feel that I am way in over my head I remember to pray and place it all back in God's hands because I believe that the ministry of supporting and empowering the most vulnerable is part of my purpose and God's will, so I leave it with him. It is such a blessing to witness the lives that have been changed, relationships healed, and achievements made because of obedience. Imagine yourself standing on a mountaintop, feeling the strength of the earth beneath, your feet, and the wind at your back. With a fierce roar, declare your intentions to the universe, knowing that you can achieve anything you set your mind to. It takes faith to jump into the new and embrace change. I believe that if you jump and take the perceived risks in line with God's will, He will not let you be ashamed nor embarrassed by the decision. The radiance and beauty of God's will is the silent symphony of starlight, weaving constellations into a tapestry of wonder that guides souls through the labyrinth of night.

Radiance is the sun's gentle kiss, painting the world in hues of warmth and wonder, igniting shadows into dances of light and shadow. It's the aura of brilliance that emanates from within, casting a luminous glow that captivates hearts and guides souls through the darkness of the night. When I hear people talk about my character, how I helped them or words that have encouraged them that I have spoken, it blows me away because I can hardly accept the credit for it. I know that every tear cried, every pain felt and every time I was buried in my pit of darkness. During the season of being hidden in darkness, God was working on me, He had a plan, and I was right where He had wanted me to be. The person that people describe sounds wise, strong, peculiar, intriguing, knowledgeable, caring, nurturing, captivating and humble. *I did not know that I was me!* The name Naomi means *beauty and pleasant* and for many years that was just words on a paper that had no weight or meaning. My heart is so full that God saw it fit to gift me with grace and mercy. As I write these words my prayer is that you accept life too and the grace afforded to you by His son Jesus Christ of Nazareth. I have danced the undignified dance of freedom many times. Knowing that I am set free, healed and delivered. Of course, I have my moments and the reality of living in this very human world blindsides me at times, however, I remember that my hope is built on nothing less than Jesus Christ and His righteousness, so I rarely lean towards people for freedom but wholly put my trust in the Maker of the heavens and the earth. I have since walked hand in hand with many on the journey of acceptance, I remember vividly a conversation between myself and a supervisee, we discussed the intersections of their life, being a woman, being black, having a diagnosis of ADHD. They were exhausted trying to fit in, to manage and prioritise their time and the competing demands. Instead, they were left with hopelessness, in a role where they were looked to for a sense of optimism.

I worked with them on developing skills in assertiveness, self-care, mindfulness and setting achievable daily goals. They share their relief in finding peace within a space which once caused them a lot of contention, they no longer found themselves eager to leave their job, only to find that the *grass was not greener on the other side*. Visualise God as a lighthouse on a stormy night, guiding lost ships safely to shore with His beacon of light. As He shines His light brightly, feel the warmth of God spreading outward, illuminating the darkness and revealing the path to self discovery for all who seek it. In 2 Corinthians 10:5, we are reminded to hold our thoughts accountable and bring them in line with the will of Christ. In doing so you will unveil your true self. Radiance is not just the sun's kiss; it is the warmth of God's spirit shining through, illuminating even the darkest corners with hope and possibility. From your dark place, just as a butterfly emerges from its cocoon, you are unveiling layers of doubt and fear, revealing the vibrant beauty God has placed within. Your journey is a masterpiece in progress, each moment a brushstroke painting a portrait of resilience and self-discovery.

Embrace the adventure ahead, knowing that every step brings you closer to soaring into a sky of endless opportunity.

Each experience, each whispered secret of your identity, is like a precious book in the vast library of your soul. As you acknowledge your true self, feel the Divine whispers guiding you towards your purpose, igniting a flame within that burns brighter than you could ever imagine. Release the weight of past burdens like a leaf drifting on an autumn breeze, allowing the winds of change to carry you towards new horizons. Your growth in Christ is like a symphony, each element coming together in perfect harmony to create a masterpiece of understanding and wholeness. Trust in the journey, knowing that every challenge is a stepping stone towards the mountaintop where your victory awaits. Remember that by aligning your thoughts with the will of Christ, you will unveil the true masterpiece of your soul.

CHAPTER SEVEN
EMBRACE AND OCCUPY

'*The Devil will try two things. One to do everything in his power to stop you from accepting eternal life. If that does not work and you take the step of faith and accept Jesus Christ as your Lord and Saviour. He wants to make you ineffective in the kingdom of God.*' excerpt from a sermon by Bishop Sean Samuel, 2009.

Does this resonate? All this time the battle was not about individuals but a wider strategy to fight against the heavens. To embrace your true purpose is to be like a blank canvas, allowing God to layer the colours of understanding, compassion, love, joy, peace, hope, wisdom, clarity and salvation. You will learn to wrap your arms around challenges because the newfound knowledge of whose you are will inspire you to see the opportunities that can often be disguised. You can start to hold on tight to dreams, those delicate treasures which keep your heart beating inanticipation and wait on the Lord with expectation of when they will be unveiled. When embracing the newfound freedom from the past weathering all ties to broken thinking. You allow yourself the opportunity to dream again. To embrace the all-encompassing idea that the version God had in mind when creating you, will give you the permission needed to occupy your space. God breathed life into possibilities and ignited a spark in your spirit that encourages, fuels, and grows and it has produced a tower of resilience within you that others will see and know the goodness of who He is. Think about warfare for a moment, usually, there is a battle plan. I like to think of this as the art of war, a strategic dance, where each move is a calculated step towards victory. Whatever you had planned for your life it is bigger than that and it is time to become strategic with decisions, conversations and connections. No moment is a coincidence but an opportunity to draw out what is inside of you and utilise it as a source of strength for the battleground.

Additionally, and not regrettably every misstep is a lesson in resilience andadaptability, so embrace the mistakes, they are an opportunity to not only remind you that you are human and rely on the Creator but also allow you to feel empathy for others' battles. Imagine your warfare as a symphony conducted by a masterful composer, where every instrument represents a facet of strategy to break curses in your community and every note a tactical decision to reclaim more ground for your family. It is an art because you learn to creatively and graciously harness the power of the spirit in you by transforming the mind and allowing God to turn adversity into opportunity, whilst weaving a tapestry of courage on the battlefield of life. Regardless of what comes your way do not move, and most definitely do not give up ground.

MASTERING THE ART OF SPIRITUAL WARFARE I love to watch films on war and enjoy the battle scenes where all of the training and strategy now is put to the test. Often there are scenes where it can seem as though the enemy is gaining ground, and the battle is lost. Especially when there are men being slaughtered on each side. It is so inspiring to see the leader of the army, the commander-in-chief look around with a moment of panic, despair and fear but then find the courage that was hidden deep down in him to fight. To remind his army to not lose ground, to dig their heels in and lock in their shields. I would often hear them shout *"shield wall"* and as they move as one instead of one thousand men, they take the background and occupy new space. No one individual could do this unless they had spent time preparing for the battle. What are you doing with your time? Are you praying, fasting, gaining knowledge and understanding by reading the Bible? Do you steal moments from this busy life to sit and meditate on the word of God? Are you proactive in learning the deep thoughts and plans of your Creator? This is the winner's mentality. There will be loss, there will be grievances and there will most definitely be a fight.

I remember a conversation that inspired me after a fight that had lasted so long that I had forgotten that I was even in a battle. It was a very brief but impactful exchange of conversation, where I had *'tongue in cheek'* said *"I have been hidden"*, as a prominent leader had shared that it seemed I was the *"shy one"*, his response to my comment referred to the Prophet Huldah, who was hidden. This comment has stayed with me and offered a new perspective and insight into the purpose and gifts that God had given to me. Huldah is a prophetess mentioned in the Bible. Her story can be found in 2 Kings 22, from verse 14 and in 2 Chronicles chapter 34 from verse 22. Prophetess Huldah emerges as a beacon of wisdom and courage in a time of uncertainty. Like a hidden gem waiting to be discovered, she embodies the essence of divine revelation and clarity. Imagine her as a guiding light amidst the shadows of doubt and confusion, her words piercing through the darkness with insight and assurance.

Huldah's purpose was to serve as a conduit for God's truth, a vessel through which His divine messages flow. Picture her as a spiritual architect, laying the foundation of faith and understanding with each prophecy she delivered. In a world where voices may falter and visions blur, Huldah stood firm as a pillar of strength, her words esonating with authority and conviction.

Through her example, you can learn the power of faithfulness and obedience, even when faced with challenges. Huldah's presence in the Bible encourages you to embrace your unique calling and trust in the guiding hand of God, knowing that He will illuminate your path and reveal His purpose in due time. Now that you are here in this place where you are no longer hidden but unveiled, how does it feel? God is unveiling a masterpiece; the grand reveal is something that happens usually once in a lifetime. A defining moment where hidden brilliance emerges from the shadows, captivating all who witness its splendour. It is the moment when the curtains part, unveiling potential and wonder, usually in this moment all starts to make sense. It is a space that invites you to step forward with confidence and embrace the beauty of your purpose that awaits. As part of the process of being unveiled, there must be a stripping away of the layers that you have used this far to make sense of the world. A removal of old ways and ideas which got you this far. I know it worked up until now, those behaviours and thoughts, but this is a new platform and God wants you to be open to change, in a way that you have never been vulnerable and open before. It is time to step into new territory, not only exist or stay there but to actually occupy the space. It is yours to take care of and protect. This has been the battle all along, to stop you from occupying what was ordained by God.

Consider this analogy, I as a writer devote myself to crafting stories that resonate deeply with readers, claiming literary territory with every word penned. Or as a skilled artist meticulously tends to their canvas, each stroke of the brush is a deliberate assertion of presence and purpose. Even envision this narrative, you the entrepreneur who fearlessly establishes their business in a competitive market, carving out a niche and thriving amidst challenges? Whatever the territory that you were born to occupy it is important that you embody the spirit of a worker who tends to their plot with dedication and care, cultivating a lush landscape of ideas, relationships, and accomplishments. Just as God nurtures each of you as plants to blossom in harmony, so too must you nurture your territory. Whether it be your career, creative pursuits, or personal endeavours, nurture them with resilience and vision. In doing so, you not only claim your space but also create a flourishing environment where your gifts can bloom and make space for someone else to blossom too. We are all connected, so what you do will in time make room for your family who have lost their way, or your friends who are looking to you and your community who may be searching for an answer. God has placed the answer within you, it has always been there. Remember, it takes one! In the face of adversity, you are encouraged to see yourself as blank canvases, allowing God to paint a masterpiece of understanding, compassion, and salvation within you. Each challenge becomes an opportunity for growth, as you learn to navigate life's battles with resilience and strategic wisdom. Just like a symphony or a dance, every decision and action is a calculated step towards victory, reclaiming ground for God's kingdom and breaking curses in your communities.

Drawing inspiration from Prophetess Huldah, you are reminded of the importance of faithfulness and obedience in fulfilling your unique calling. Her example encourages you to trust in God's timing and purpose, even when faced with uncertainty. As you step into the unveiling of your true selves, you are urged to embrace change and occupy the space ordained for you by God. In essence, this book serves as a rallying cry to embrace your identity and purpose, knowing that every moment, decision, and connection has the power to shape your destiny and fulfill God's plan for your life.

Dear Reader,

I invite you to **COME OUT OF HIDING**.

I eagerly await your reintroduction,

Author.

Printed in Great Britain
by Amazon